MARSEILLE TRAVEL GUIDE 2023

Discover the Treasures of the French Riviera

Angelia J. Rea

Copyright © Angelia J. Rea 2023

All rights reserved. No part of this publication may be reproduced, distributed, or transmitted in any form or by any means, including photocopying, recording, or other electronic or mechanical methods, without the prior written permission of the publisher, except in the case of brief quotations embodied in critical reviews and certain other noncommercial uses permitted by copyright law.

TABLE OF CONTENT

CHAPTER 1: INTRODUCTION.................................7
    Marseille Brief History.. 11
    Weather Situation In Marseille....................... 14
    Architectural Highlights................................... 17
    Culture And People Of Marseille....................20

CHAPTER 2: ARE YOU PLANNING A TRIP TO MARSEILLE?.. 24
    Visiting Marseille On A Budget........................24
    What To Bring Along On Your Trip.................. 26
    Getting Around Marseille................................29
    The Best Way To Get There............................32
    The Top 20 Reasons To Visit Marseille........... 35
    Top 5 Marseille Events To Attend...................39
    Children and Marseille.................................... 42

CHAPTER 3: MARSEILLE ACCOMMODATION.46
    Tips For Locating And Reserving Lodging...... 46
    Recommendations For Various Budget Levels When Visiting Marseille...................................49
    5 Expensive Hotels to Stay At While Visiting Marseille...52
    5 Mid-Range Hotels To Stay At While Visiting Marseille...55
    5 Low-Cost Hotels To Stay In When Visiting Marseille...57

CHAPTER 4: MARSEILLE DINING AND DRINKING... 60
    A Look At The Marseille Culinary Scene.........60
    Popular Restaurant And Bistros......................63

10 Must-Try Marseille's Delectable Cuisine.... 66
How To Get Inexpensive Meals During Your Stay............ 72

CHAPTER 5: MARSEILLE SIGHTSEEING AND OUTDOOR ACTIVITIES............ 76

Marseille's Top 15 Attractions............ 76
Discounts And Information On Sightseeing Passes............ 80
Sailing And Boat Tours In Marseille............ 82
Beaches And Water Sports In Marseille......... 84
Hiking And Treking In Calanques............ 86
Cycling Routes............ 88
Itinerary For 3 Days............ 92
Itinerary For 7 Days............ 96

CHAPTER 6: MARSEILLE SHOPPING............ 102

Overview Of The Marseille Shopping Scene 102
Suggestions For Marseille Shopping............ 104
10 Must-Buy Souvenirs............ 105
Tips For Saving Money And Avoiding Tourist Traps............ 112

CHAPTER 7: MARSEILLE'S NIGHTLIFE IS EXCITING............ 118

Live Music Venues............ 119
Nightclubs and Dance Spots............ 122
Theater and Performing Art............ 124
Bars And Pubs............ 127

CHAPTER 8: RECOGNIZING FOREIGN TRANSACTION FEES............ 132

Avoid Paying Cell Phone Roaming Fees...... 133
Map Download For Offline Use............ 136
Learn The Fundamentals Of The Language. 139

The Cost Of Cash At The Airport Is High	141
CONCLUSION	**143**
Tips For A Memorable Trip	143
Travel Advice And Aditional Resourses	148
Appendix	**151**
Maps of Marseille	151

CHAPTER 1: INTRODUCTION

Chloe, an adventurous traveller with an insatiable wanderlust, set out on a voyage to this captivating location to immerse herself in the rich fabric of its past and present. Chloe's Marseille journey promised to be nothing short of a transforming adventure, drawn by the pull of its unique past, breathtaking scenery, and gastronomic delights. Chloe was intrigued by Marseille's buzzing energy and seamless blending of old and new from the moment she arrived. The architectural marvels of the city's ancient roots, such as the awe-inspiring Basilique Notre-Dame de la

Garde, give panoramic views of the city and the dazzling Mediterranean beyond. Wanderlust compelled her to visit the charming Vieux-Port, where colourful fishing boats bobbed elegantly amid the calm waves and modern waterfront restaurants beckoned with the promise of wonderful seafood delights.

Chloe explored the city's diverse neighbourhoods, each with its own particular character and charm, in addition to historic sites and scenic surroundings. Her heart was stolen by the bohemian air of the Le Panier district, with its small cobblestone alleyways and unique art culture. She got lost in the maze of streets, discovering hidden treasures like local ateliers and quaint boutiques.

Chloe found herself in the vibrant Cours Julien as the sun set, where street musicians filled the air with lovely tunes and laughter echoed from lively cafes and bars. She savoured the renowned Provençal food, drinking Pastis and savouring bouillabaisse, a traditional fisherman's stew that encompassed Mediterranean flavours.

Chloe embraced the Marseille atmosphere by taking a boat cruise to the picturesque Calanques, limestone cliffs, and turquoise bays that spread down the coastline. The astounding grandeur of Mother Nature's masterpiece left her humbled and speechless.

However, Chloe's Marseille trip was more than just sightseeing and gastronomic indulgences; it was about interacting with the inhabitants, hearing their tales, and understanding the city's pulsating heart. The Marseillais' great hospitality invited her to engage in spirited talks, each experience adding a new layer of understanding to this multifaceted city.

As her trip to Marseille progressed, Chloe learned that the city's fascination stretched beyond its superficial allure. It was a location where civilizations collided, where tradition and modernity coexisted, and where history and modern life blended. Marseille had left an indelible imprint on her psyche, leaving her with memories to last a lifetime and a wish to return to this intriguing seaside port city.

Marseille Brief History

Marseille, located in southeastern France, has a rich and dynamic history that dates back over 2,600 years. It is one of Europe's oldest continually inhabited cities, having been founded by the ancient Greeks approximately 600 BC. Originally called as Massalia, the city swiftly grew into an important Mediterranean port and trading centre.

Marseille had several obstacles and developments throughout the centuries that followed. During the Roman conquest of Gaul in 49 BC, it fell under Roman administration. The Romans left an unmistakable mark on the city's architecture and culture, as seen by facilities such as the Roman docks, which are now submerged beneath the contemporary Vieux-Port (Old Port).

Marseille was subjected to numerous invasions during the mediaeval period, including those by the Visigoths and the Moors. It did, however, preserve its strategic importance as a maritime hub. Marseille became an important actor in European trade throughout the 16th century, owing to its vast contacts to the Orient.

In addition, the city was devastated by the Great Plague of Marseille in 1720, which resulted in a large loss of life and an economic collapse. Marseille, on the other hand, recovered and continued to expand as a significant port city.

The completion of the Suez Canal in the nineteenth century increased Marseille's commercial significance, making it a gateway for trade between Europe, Africa, and the Far East. Industrialization accelerated the city's growth by attracting a diversified stream of individuals from many places.

Marseille experienced severe obstacles during World War II, as it was occupied by the Nazis. It did, however, play an important role in the French Resistance and, after the war, reclaimed its status as a significant Mediterranean port and a flourishing cultural centre.

Marseille is now France's second-largest city and an important centre for commerce, tourism, and culture. Its ancient attractions, cosmopolitan culture, and scenic surroundings continue to draw people from all over the world, demonstrating the city's lasting and vibrant history.

Weather Situation In Marseille

Marseille, a lovely port city on France's southern coast, has a Mediterranean climate, with moderate, wet winters and scorching, dry summers. The city has a good environment for much of the year, making it a popular tourist and resident destination.

Temperatures in Marseille normally range from 5°C to 13°C (41°F to 55°F) during the winter months (December to February). Although snowfall is uncommon during this time of year, there may be a few cold and rainy days.

Spring (March to May) offers warmer weather, with average temperatures ranging from 10°C to 19°C (50°F to 66°F). This is a wonderful season in general, as the city comes alive with blooming flowers and greenery.

Summer in Marseille is hot and dry, with typical temperatures ranging from 28°C to 31°C (82°F to 88°F). Heatwaves are typical during this time of year, and visitors can escape the heat by visiting one of the city's many beaches.

Temperatures range from 16°C to 23°C (61°F to 73°F) during autumn (September to November). As the season advances, rain becomes more regular, giving much-needed water to the region after the dry summer months.

It's important to note that weather patterns might change from year to year.

Architectural Highlights

- **The Vieux-Port (Old Port)** is located in the centre of Marseille and is a historic harbour that has served as the city's focal point for centuries. Visitors can marvel at the colourful facades of old buildings along the waterfront, many of which have been turned into vibrant cafes, restaurants, and boutiques. The neighbourhood emanates a pleasant, authentic vibe that captures the essence of Marseille's past.

- **Notre-Dame de la Garde Basilica:** The Notre-Dame de la Garde Basilica, perched on the city's highest point, is an iconic symbol of Marseille. This magnificent Neo-Byzantine edifice, embellished with colourful mosaics, provides beautiful views of the city and the Mediterranean Sea. It has religious importance and is a must-see for its architectural splendour.
- **Le Corbusier's Cité Radieuse:** The Cité Radieuse, designed by renowned architect Le Corbusier, is a pioneering example of modernist architecture. This "vertical garden city" apartment complex, completed in 1952, has a striking concrete façade and an innovative design that prioritises practicality and community spaces.
- **The Museum of European and Mediterranean Civilizations**

(MuCEM) is a modern architectural wonder. It is a fusion of traditional and modern designs, with a sleek, latticed concrete outer shell that contrasts well with the old Fort Saint-Jean, to which it is linked by a footbridge.

- **Palais Longchamp:** Built in the nineteenth century, this spectacular monument commemorates Marseille's water delivery system. The Palais Longchamp is a magnificent neoclassical complex that houses a colossal fountain, a museum of fine arts, and a natural history museum.

Culture And People Of Marseille

Marseille's culture is a fascinating blend of historic traditions, Mediterranean influences, and current cosmopolitan flare as the country's second-largest city and one of France's oldest cities.

Marseille residents, known as Marseillais, are extremely proud of their city's distinct identity. The population is a multicultural melting pot with significant ties to Mediterranean, North African, and Corsican groups. This diversity is reflected in the city's gastronomic offerings, which include bouillabaisse, the classic fisherman's stew, as well as couscous and other North African specialties. The vibrant markets, such as the Old Port (Vieux Port) and Noailles, highlight the colourful mix of cultures, as well as the people' proclivity for engaging in passionate talks with traders and visitors alike.

Marseille's culture is inextricably linked to its nautical history. The city's pulsing heart remains the Old Port, a historic harbour dating back to antiquity. Visitors may see fishermen at work, sail boats dotting the azure waterways, and take leisurely strolls along the waterfront promenades. In addition, the port holds a variety of cultural events, open-air concerts, and festivals that showcase the region's music, dancing, and art.

Sports, particularly football, hold a special place in Marseillais hearts. The city is home to Olympique de Marseille, one of France's most famous football clubs, and the Stade Vélodrome stadium is packed with enthusiastic fans on match days.

Another important component of Marseille's culture is its ancient architecture. The Notre-Dame de la Garde Basilica, perched on a hill, provides beautiful views of the city and the sea. The characteristic "Panier" sector is distinguished by small, meandering lanes lined with colourful buildings, a tribute to the city's ancient legacy.

CHAPTER 2: ARE YOU PLANNING A TRIP TO MARSEILLE?

Visiting Marseille On A Budget

First and foremost, while travelling on a budget, lodging is an important consideration. Look for low-cost hotels and hostels, or consider alternatives such as Airbnb. Staying just outside of the city centre can also help you save money on lodging while still providing easy access to public transit.

Walking is one of the greatest ways to discover Marseille. Walking through the city's different neighbourhoods, historic alleys, and attractive squares is a terrific way to absorb in the local vibe without spending a dollar.

Marseille's cultural scene is also easily accessible without breaking the bank. Many museums, like the Museum of European and Mediterranean Civilizations (MUCEM), offer free admission on certain days or during specific hours. Furthermore, the city's historic landmarks, such as the Notre-Dame de la Garde cathedral and Fort Saint-Jean, are free to visit from the outside.

Exploring Marseille's colourful markets is not only inexpensive, but also a fascinating opportunity to learn about the local culture. The seafood market at the Old Port and the Noailles market are great places to sample the city's flavours and obtain fresh produce at cheap costs.

Because of Marseille's coastal location, you may enjoy the beautiful beaches without spending a fortune. Pack a picnic and head to Calanques National Park to hike, swim and enjoy the natural beauty of the limestone cliffs and blue waters.

Finally, use Marseille's enormous public transport system, which includes buses, trams and ferries, to get around the city and its environs on the cheap.

What To Bring Along On Your Trip

- **Comfortable Walking Shoes:** Marseille's picturesque streets and hilly terrain need the use of comfortable walking shoes. Whether you're strolling through the lively Le Panier neighbourhood or ascending to the Basilique Notre-Dame de la Garde, dependable footwear will keep you going.
- **Sun Protection:** Because the Mediterranean environment may be harsh, bring sunscreen, sunglasses, and a wide-brimmed hat to protect yourself from the sun's rays while relaxing on

gorgeous beaches or sipping coffee at outdoor cafés.

- **Travel adaptor:** Bring a compatible travel adaptor for France's European-style power outlets to keep your electrical gadgets charged.
- **While many locals speak English**, having a rudimentary command of French phrases would be appreciated and can help you traverse less touristy places.
- **Marseille is a beautiful city with stunning views**, antique architecture, and dynamic street scenes. Don't forget to photograph or videotape those priceless moments.
- **Beach Essentials**: If you plan to visit the beaches, bring a swimsuit, a beach towel and possibly snorkelling equipment to experience the Mediterranean Sea's underwater splendour.

- **Reusable Water Bottle:** Carry a reusable water bottle with you on your sightseeing expeditions to stay hydrated. You may refill it at any of the city's public fountains.
- **Travel Journal:** The rich history and diverse culture of Marseille may inspire you to write down your ideas and experiences. A travel notebook is a fantastic method to capture your journey and build memories that will last a lifetime.
- **A modest daypack** will come in handy for transporting your things as you visit the numerous sights in Marseille.

Getting Around Marseille

- **The public transport system** in the city is efficient and well-developed, making it simple for visitors to get around. The metro, which connects significant districts like as the Old Port, the St. Charles train station, and prominent attractions, serves as the network's backbone. In addition, the metro is supplemented with a substantial bus network that covers places not accessible by train. When hopping between attractions, purchasing a multi-day pass or a Marseille City Pass might save you time and money.

- **Consider taking a boat trip** along the coast for a more scenic and leisurely way to travel. Boats leave from the Old Port on a regular basis, providing stunning views of the city skyline and the dazzling Mediterranean Sea. Some boat tours even take you to surrounding islands such as the Frioul Archipelago and Château d'If, which were made famous by Alexandre Dumas' novel "The Count of Monte Cristo."

- **Cycling** is a good alternative in Marseille if you prefer a more active experience. The city has a growing network of bike lanes, and many businesses provide affordable bike rentals. Biking allows you to discover hidden gems and attractive neighbourhoods at your own speed.
- **Walking** remains one of the greatest ways to discover Marseille, especially for shorter distances or to immerse oneself in the local ambiance. Cafes, boutiques and local markets line the city's winding alleyways, beckoning you to wander and savour the Mediterranean lifestyle.
- **Taxis and ride-sharing** services are available, however they are typically more expensive than public

transportation options. Save them for times when you need a quick and easy ride or when exploring the nearby area.

Getting around Marseille is a breeze, whether you utilise the metro, buses, boats, bikes, or your own two feet. Explore the streets of this eclectic city, discovering the cultural tapestry that makes Marseille a true Mediterranean treasure.

The Best Way To Get There

- **By Air:** Flying to Marseille Provence Airport (MRS) from an overseas destination or a remote place is the most time-efficient alternative. The airport has direct flights to key cities in Europe and other continents. To get to the city centre, you can take a shuttle, cab, or public transportation from the airport.

- **By Train**: Taking the train to Marseille is a fantastic option for a scenic journey that is also environmentally sustainable. The French high-speed train network (TGV) serves the city, with direct links to Paris, Lyon, and other major towns. Marseille's train terminals are centrally positioned, allowing for easy access to many attractions.
- **Driving to Marseille** might be a great experience if you want freedom and want to explore the neighbouring regions. The city is well-connected to the French highway network, and the roads are generally in good condition. However, be mindful of traffic and parking issues in the city centre.
- **Long-distance buses** are a cost-effective solution for budget-conscious travellers. Several bus companies run routes to

Marseille from nearby cities as well as several foreign destinations.

- **By Sea:** If you're arriving from a neighbouring Mediterranean destination or seeking for a one-of-a-kind vacation experience, take a ferry to Marseille's Old Port. Marseille is connected by ferry to Corsica, Sardinia, and North Africa.

The Top 20 Reasons To Visit Marseille

1. **The Old Port**, the city's beating centre, is a lively waterfront district overflowing with restaurants, pubs, and street performers.
2. **Visit historical** sites such as Notre-Dame de la Garde, Château d'If, and the Abbey of St. Victor.

3. **Calanques National Park**: This natural beauty, only a short drive from the city, provides stunning climbs and clean blue lakes.
4. **Art & Culture**: The MuCEM, MAC, and several galleries across the city showcase Marseille's strong artistic sector.
5. **Food & Cuisine:** From fresh seafood to classic bouillabaisse, savour wonderful Mediterranean cuisine.
6. **Street marketplaces**: Visit marketplaces like Marché de la Joliette and Marché du Prado to immerse yourself in local culture.
7. **Festivals**: Throughout the year, Marseille holds a variety of festivals honouring anything from music and cinema to gastronomy and art.
8. **Beaches**: Take advantage of Marseille's exquisite beaches, such as Plage du

Prado and Plage des Catalans, with their sandy coasts and mild waves.

9. **Boat Tours**: Take a boat excursion around the coast, explore surrounding islands, or enjoy a sunset sail.
10. **Activities** fans may attend a football match at the renowned Stade Vélodrome or participate in aquatic activities like as sailing and diving.
11. **Admire a varied range of architectural styles**, from ancient ruins to modern wonders.
12. **Retail**: In Marseille's retail areas, you'll find unique shops, high-end fashion stores, and local crafts.
13. **Friendly Locals**: Enjoy the warm welcome of Marseille residents known as "Marseillais."
14. **Music and nighttime**: Take advantage of the vibrant nighttime scene, which

includes live music venues, pubs, and clubs.

15. **Street Art**: Explore the city streets for spectacular street art and murals.
16. Wine Tasting: Visit surrounding vineyards and sample delectable Provencal wines.
17. **Les Docks** is a redeveloped warehouse neighbourhood that currently houses chic restaurants, boutiques, and cultural venues.
18. **Charming Neighbourhoods**: Each neighbourhood, from Le Panier to Cours Julien, has its own distinct personality and charm.
19. **Marseille's varied population** contributes to its strong cultural variety and impacts its cuisine and traditions.
20. **Marseille has a Mediterranean climate** with moderate winters and balmy

summers, making it an ideal year-round resort.

Top 5 Marseille Events To Attend

1. **Printemps du Cinéma, held in March**, is a cinematic spectacle that honours the art of filmmaking. During this festival, movie theatres across the city provide low admission rates, inviting both residents and visitors to experience the latest cinematic innovations. This programme has something for everyone, from critically acclaimed worldwide films to thought-provoking indie movies.
2. **Summer - Marseille Jazz Festival**: The Marseille Jazz Festival, held in July, gathers top-tier jazz performers from throughout the world. The festival, held in gorgeous locales such as parks and open-air venues, provides a

one-of-a-kind opportunity to experience mesmerising performances while basking in the pleasant summer wind. Whether you're a jazz fanatic or simply seeking to try something new, this event will leave you with wonderful musical memories.

3. **Autumn - La Fête de la Gastronomie**: In September, foodies celebrate as La Fête de la Gastronomie, a festival of French gastronomic pleasures, takes place. Marseille's unique culinary culture comes to life with a range of gourmet events, food tastings, and cooking classes highlighting the best of the region's cuisine. You'll be able to sample the finest of Marseille's gourmet offerings, from classic bouillabaisse to exquisite pastries.

4. **When winter approaches**, the city changes into a winter wonderland, with

charming Christmas markets popping up in various neighbourhoods. These markets include attractive wooden chalets decorated with dazzling lights that sell homemade items, decorations, and seasonal delicacies. Drink mulled wine, eat roasted chestnuts, and get into the holiday atmosphere while shopping for unique items.

5. **MuCEM Exhibitions Throughout the Year**: The Museum of European and Mediterranean Civilizations (MuCEM) provides enthralling exhibitions throughout the year. MuCEM, with its contemporary building near the Old Port's entrance, highlights the history, art, and culture of the Mediterranean area. There is always an exciting exhibit ready to increase your knowledge and awareness of the world no matter when you visit Marseille.

Children and Marseille

The city's marine heritage is one of its most appealing attractions for youngsters. The busy Old Port, surrounded with colourful fishing boats and yachts, transforms into a wonderland for young explorers. Children may enjoy the salty wind and the stunning vistas of the Mediterranean Sea, stimulating their imaginations with fantasies of marine adventures.

Marseille's international ambiance captivates young minds with a tapestry of languages, traditions, and food beyond the waterfront. Children find lovely boutiques, art galleries, and cafés as they meander through the maze-like alleyways of Le Panier, the city's oldest area, delivering sensory joys and cultural insights.

Marseille also has a multitude of family-friendly activities, such as interactive museums like the MuCEM (Museum of

European and Mediterranean Civilisations) and the La Vieille Charité, which provide engaging displays that pique visitors' interest and encourage learning. The Grand Aquarium de Marseille, the city's famed aquarium, takes youngsters on an underwater voyage, showing marine life from the Mediterranean and beyond. Calanques National Park welcomes outdoor adventurers with its beautiful rivers and limestone cliffs, giving a natural playground for exploration, hiking, and picnics. Children may connect with nature, learning to appreciate its beauty as well as its fragility.

Furthermore, Marseille's passion for sports, particularly football, unites the community by allowing youngsters to engage and share in the excitement of the game. The city's stadiums are packed with applauding supporters, promoting a feeling of community and a love of sportsmanship.

CHAPTER 3: MARSEILLE ACCOMMODATION

Tips For Locating And Reserving Lodging

- **Investigate neighbourhoods**: Marseille has a broad range of neighbourhoods, each of which offers a distinct experience. Before booking a reservation, investigate the several regions to select the one that best matches your interests and preferences. The Old Port (Vieux Port) is suitable for a lively setting, but Le Panier offers a wonderful historic ambience.
- **Set a budget:** Determine your hotel budget early on. Marseille offers a wide choice of accommodation options, from luxury hotels to low-cost hostels. Setting

a budget can allow you to reduce your alternatives and avoid overpaying.

- **Use online platforms**: To browse a variety of housing possibilities, use hotel booking websites and online travel agents. You may use these sites to compare costs, read reviews, and look at images of suitable hotels.
- **Try alternatives to hotels**: While hotels are a popular option, try vacation rentals, guesthouses, or boutique hotels. These options can deliver one-of-a-kind experiences and are frequently more personalised.
- **Check for closeness to attractions**: Make sure your selected hotel is close to the attractions you intend to see. The public transit system in Marseille is efficient, but staying within walking distance of significant sights might save

you time and improve your entire experience.

- **Read the following reviews and ratings**: Take note of guest reviews and ratings, since they give useful information about the quality of service, cleanliness, and overall client happiness. Look for lodgings that have received consistent favourable evaluations.
- **Plan ahead of time:** Marseille is a popular location, particularly during high tourist seasons. Book your hotel well in advance to get the greatest pricing and availability.
- **Contact the lodging directly**: Consider contacting the accommodation directly if you have special demands or require extra information. They can answer any questions and perhaps provide special offers.

Recommendations For Various Budget Levels When Visiting Marseille

- **Budget Travellers:**

Don't worry if you're on a limited budget; Marseille has lots of reasonable choices to discover and enjoy. Consider staying in one of the city's budget-friendly hostels or guesthouses. For cheap yet wonderful lunches, go to local markets and street food carts. Picnics at parks or beaches are a great way to take in the scenery without breaking the bank.

Visit the Old Port (Vieux Port) and walk along the gorgeous harbour for free. Discover the city's ancient area, Le Panier, with its twisting lanes, lovely stores, and street art. On the first Sunday of each month, several museums provide free entrance, so plan your trips accordingly. Don't miss the majestic

Notre-Dame de la Garde, which offers free panoramic views over Marseille.

- **Mid-Range Travellers:**

If you have a little more money to spend, stay in comfortable mid-range hotels or elegant boutique lodgings. Dine at local bistros and seafood restaurants, which provide exceptional value for money, to experience Marseille's unique culinary scene.

Take a boat ride to the Calanques National Park to experience the magnificent limestone cliffs, blue seas, and isolated beaches. Join one of the city's guided walking tours to learn more about its history and culture. Visit the MuCEM (Museum of European and Mediterranean Civilizations) and the Palais Longchamp, both of which demand modest admission fees for an educational experience.

- **Luxury Travellers:**

Marseille does not disappoint those looking for a premium vacation. Stay in premium hotels or trendy boutique lodgings with views of the Mediterranean Sea to pamper yourself. Fine eating at Michelin-starred restaurants or trendy gourmet cafes is available.

Discover the beauty of the coast in luxury with private boat charters. Book customised guided excursions to customise your discovery of Marseille's hidden jewels. Enjoy spa days and relaxation at high-end wellness centres.

5 Expensive Hotels to Stay At While Visiting Marseille

1. **Le Petit Nice Passedat** This hotel is located in Maldormé, a beach area within a few minutes' drive from the city centre. It boasts two Michelin stars, and its restaurant is regarded as one of the best in Marseille. The hotel is lavish in and of itself, with big rooms and suites, a

rooftop pool, and a spa. Prices begin around €400 per night.

2. **Hôtel Dieu Intercontinental Marseille.** This hotel is built in a beautifully renovated former 18th-century hospital. It lies in the city centre, adjacent to the Old Port and the Canebière. There is a rooftop pool, a spa, and two restaurants in the hotel. Prices begin about €500 per night.

3. **Sofitel Marseille Vieux Port.** This hotel is directly on the Old Port and has breathtaking views of the city. It features two restaurants, a rooftop bar, and a spa. The accommodations are large and beautiful, and the service is outstanding. Prices begin around €350 per night.

4. **C2 Hotel.** This hotel is in the fashionable Panier sector and is ideal for visitors seeking a more boutique experience. The rooms are sleek and modern, and the

hotel includes a rooftop patio with spectacular city views. Prices begin around €250 per night.
5. **nhow Marseille.** This hotel is in the Euromed sector and is an excellent alternative for anyone seeking a modern and elegant hotel. The rooms are large and well-appointed, and the hotel offers a rooftop pool and bar. Prices begin around €200 per night.

5 Mid-Range Hotels To Stay At While Visiting Marseille

1. **Mercure Marseille Centre Vieux Port**. This hotel is in the city centre, just a short walk from the Old Port and the Canebière. It offers a rooftop patio with spectacular city views, a bar and a restaurant. The accommodations are large and comfy, and the service is

outstanding. Prices begin around €150 per night.

2. **Ibis Marseille Centre Gare Saint-Charles**. This hotel is conveniently positioned near the train station, making it an excellent alternative for travellers arriving by train. It is just a short stroll to the Old Port and the Canebière. The hotel offers a bar and a restaurant, as well as contemporary and well-equipped rooms. Prices begin about €100 per night.

3. **Mama Shelter Marseille.** This hotel is located in the fashionable Panier sector and is an excellent alternative for people seeking a more distinctive experience. The rooms are sleek and modern, and the hotel includes a rooftop patio with spectacular city views. There is also a bar and a restaurant on the premises. Prices begin about €120 per night.

4. **Hotel du Nord**. This hotel is in the Old Port neighbourhood and is ideal for visitors seeking a genuine Marseille experience. The rooms are tiny but nice, and there is a wonderful courtyard garden at the hotel. There is also a bar and a restaurant on the premises. Prices begin about €100 per night.
5. **Golden Tulip Marseille Castellane**. This hotel is in the Castellane area, which is a little distance from the city centre but still easily accessible. It has a rooftop pool, as well as a bar and a restaurant. The accommodations are large and comfy, and the service is outstanding. Prices begin about €130 per night.

5 Low-Cost Hotels To Stay In When Visiting Marseille

1. **Budget Ibis Marseille Vieux Port.** This hotel is in the city centre, just a short walk from the Old Port and the Canebière. The rooms are tiny yet pleasant, and the decor is basic but efficient. On-site, there is a bar and a restaurant. Prices begin about €50 per night.
2. **Lemon Hotel Plan De Campagne Marseille.** This hotel is located in the septèmes-les-Vallons neighbourhood, about 15 minutes from the city centre. It provides modest accommodations with common bathrooms, free Wi-Fi, and parking. Prices begin about €50 per night.
3. **Hotel F1 Marseille Provence.** This hotel is located just outside of Marseille

in the village of Les Pennes-Mirabeau. It provides simple rooms with free Wi-Fi and parking. Prices begin around €35 per night.

4. **Hôtel Des Moulins**. This hotel is located in Allauch, approximately 20 minutes from the city centre. It has bright, comfortable rooms with free Wi-Fi and a garden. Prices begin around €60 per night.

5. **Staycity Aparthotels Centre Vieux Port**: Located in the centre of the Old Port, this aparthotel provides an excellent starting point for exploring the city. Apartments are self-contained, allowing you to make your own meals and save money. Prices begin around €70 per night.

CHAPTER 4: MARSEILLE DINING AND DRINKING

A Look At The Marseille Culinary Scene

The city's unique culinary options have earned it a reputation as a gourmet destination, attracting foodies from across the world.

Because of its maritime setting, seafood takes centre stage in Marseille's culinary. Many restaurants and seafood markets serve freshly caught fish, luscious mussels, and soft octopus. Bouillabaisse, a classic fish stew, is possibly the most famous dish to come from this port city. This rich and savoury soup, made with a variety of fish, shellfish, saffron, and local herbs, has become associated with Marseille cuisine.

Marseille's North African background has greatly affected its gastronomic environment, in addition to seafood. Because of the city's closeness to North Africa, fragrant spices and unique ingredients have merged. From fragrant couscous to savoury tagines, these meals have captured the hearts and palates of both Marseille locals and visitors. The busy Arab marketplaces, such as the Noailles Market, are a treasure mine of ingredients that provide insight into the city's cultural tapestry.

A walk through Marseille's ancient town, known as Le Panier, exposes an abundance of lovely boulangeries and patisseries. The city's French bakeries provide a scrumptious selection of crusty baguettes, buttery croissants, and exquisite pastries. These delectable pastries are ideal for a relaxing afternoon coffee at a charming café.

The importance of local produce markets in defining Marseille's culinary scene cannot be overstated. The Marchés de la Joliette and de la Plaine are brimming with vibrant displays of fresh fruits and vegetables, cheeses, and cured meats. This emphasis on locally obtained foods means that the city's cuisine stays true to its farm-to-table roots, emphasising freshness and quality.

Marseille has also witnessed an increase in contemporary and inventive restaurants that combine traditional skills with new culinary trends in recent years. Acclaimed chefs have begun to push the envelope, mixing traditional Marseille flavours with worldwide influences to create a dynamic fusion cuisine that continues to enchant customers.

Popular Restaurant And Bistros

- **AM Par Alexandre Mazzia:** Chef Alexandre Mazzia, who has two Michelin stars, runs this restaurant. The menu changes periodically, but anticipate unique and imaginative meals that highlight the finest of local The prix fixe meals begin at €180.

- **L'Épuisette**: This restaurant specialises in seafood and always has the catch of the day on the menu. The restaurant's location on a dock facing the Mediterranean Sea is extremely stunning. Appetisers begin at €18, main dishes begin at €30, and desserts begin at €15.
- **Le Petit Nice**: This is one of Marseille's most well-known restaurants, with three Michelin stars. The menu combines traditional French fare with a contemporary touch.
- **La Maison Rose**: This wonderful ancient home in the centre of Marseille houses the restaurant La Maison Rose. The menu consists of typical Provençal fare, and the service is exceptional. Appetisers begin at €12,

main dishes begin at €22, and desserts begin at €10.

- **Chez Fonfon**: A local favourite, this restaurant is noted for its substantial and cheap cuisine. The cuisine consists of traditional French bistro dishes, and the wine selection is substantial. Appetisers begin at €9, main dishes begin at €18, and desserts begin at €6.
- **Bistrot des Dames**: This restaurant serves unique healthful cuisine made using fresh ingredients. The ambiance is sleek and casual, and the service is exceptional.
- **Nomade** delivers sophisticated Mediterranean cuisine with an emphasis on fresh fish and vegetables. The food changes with the seasons, and the wine selection is large..
- **Réjane**: This restaurant gives a flavour of Provence with classic meals like

ratatouille and bouillabaisse on the menu. The atmosphere is nice, and the service is kind..

- **La Cantine du Panier**: This restaurant is ideal for those on a tight budget. The menu provides typical French bistro dishes with ample quantities. Appetisers begin at €14, main dishes begin at €25, and desserts begin at €12.

10 Must-Try Marseille's Delectable Cuisine

1. **Bouillabaisse**: This is Marseille's most renowned dish, and it's a must-try for any tourist. Bouillabaisse is a fish stew prepared from several types of fish, shellfish, and vegetables. It's usually accompanied by croutons and rouille, a spicy mayonnaise sauce. Price: €25-€40.

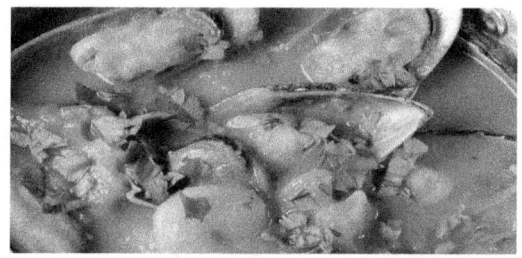

2. **Pan bagnat**: A salad sandwich filled with tuna, anchovies, tomatoes, onions, olives, and hard-boiled eggs. It is usually served on a baguette or ciabatta bun. Price: €10-€15.

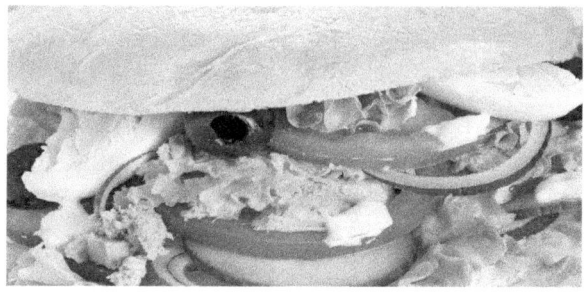

3. **Aïoli** is a garlic mayonnaise that is traditionally served with boiled potatoes, salt fish, or vegetables. It's a popular condiment in Provence, and it's also used in other recipes like salade aoli. Price: €5-€10.

4. **Lamb Provençal**: This is a lamb stew flavoured with a variety of herbs and spices. It is commonly served with potatoes or rice. Price: €20-€30.

5. **Couscous**: A North African meal prepared of semolina noodles, veggies, and either meat or fish. Couscous comes in a variety of flavours, but the most popular in Marseille is lamb couscous. Price: €15-€25.

6. **Pizza**: Marseille has some of France's greatest pizza. Pizzas are often created using fresh, locally sourced ingredients and baked in wood-fired ovens. Price: €10-€20.

7. **Tapas** are tiny, savoury meals often served as an appetiser or snack. Tapas come in a variety of flavours, but anchovies, olives, cheese, and cured meats are among the most popular in Marseille. Tapas range in price from €2 to €5.

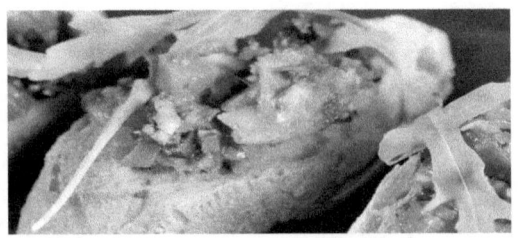

8. **Soupe de pistou**: This is a vegetable soup cooked with tomatoes, onions, garlic, basil, and olive oil. It's usually accompanied by croutons and grated Parmesan cheese. Price: €10-€15.

9. **Fougasse**: A sort of flatbread flavoured with olive oil, herbs, and spices. It's usually served as an appetiser or snack, although it may also be used to build sandwiches. Price: €5-€10.

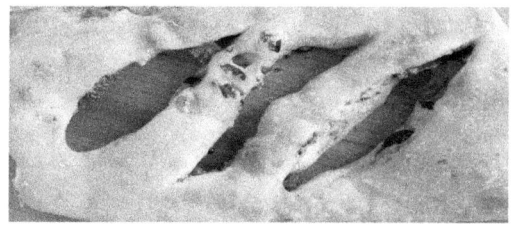

10. **Beignets** are fried pastry usually filled with custard, chocolate, or fruit. They're a popular delicacy in Marseille, and they're usually topped with powdered sugar. Price per beignet: €2-€5.

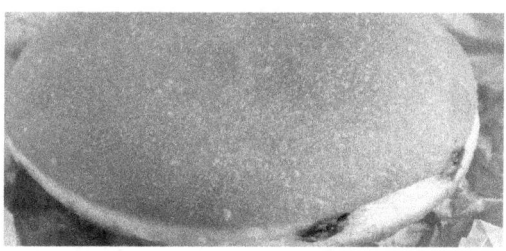

How To Get Inexpensive Meals During Your Stay

- **Street Food:** Marseille has a plethora of street food sellers and marketplaces where you may get cheap and tasty meals. One of the local sellers will sell you a delicious panisse (chickpea fritter) or a savoury socca (chickpea pancake).

- **Boulangeries & Patisseries**: For freshly made baguettes, pastries, and sandwiches at moderate costs, visit a local bakery. A croissant or pain au chocolat with a cup of coffee may make for a delicious and inexpensive breakfast.
- **Menu du Jour**: Many restaurants in Marseille provide a "Menu du Jour" or daily set menu that includes an appetiser, main dish, and dessert for a fixed fee. This is a wonderful way to have a full supper without breaking the bank.
- **Local Markets**: Visit Marseille's bustling outdoor markets, such as Marché Noailles, to sample seasonal fruit, cheeses, and cured meats. A picnic-style lunch may be put together for a fraction of the price of eating out.

- **Le Panier**: Explore the historic area of Le Panier for tiny cafés and bistros serving cheap regional food in a picturesque setting.
- **Food Trucks**: Look for food trucks dotted across the city. They frequently provide wonderful and reasonably priced delicacies, providing for a quick and pleasant supper on the run.
- **Choose eateries that provide sharing platters or tapas-style food**. Sharing multiple small meals with friends or family is not only economical, but also a terrific opportunity to try new flavours.
- **Waterfront refreshments**: While admiring the magnificent Marseille coastline, pick up some inexpensive refreshments from local merchants along the waterfront, such as fresh seafood, sandwiches, or ice cream.

CHAPTER 5:MARSEILLE SIGHTSEEING AND OUTDOOR ACTIVITIES

Marseille's Top 15 Attractions

1. **The heart of the city, Vieux Port (Old Port)**, is teeming with fishing boats, luxury yachts, and vibrant waterfront cafes.
2. **Notre-Dame de la Garde Basilica:** Perched on a hill, this historic basilica provides spectacular panoramic views of Marseille and the surrounding countryside.
3. **Le Panier**: Marseille's oldest neighbourhood, Le Panier emits a

bohemian vibe with its small lanes, art studios, and fashionable stores.

4. **MuCEM**: The Museum of European and Mediterranean Civilizations presents interesting exhibits that highlight the region's history and cultural heritage.

5. **Château d'If**: This infamous island fortification, which appears in Alexandre Dumas' "The Count of Monte Cristo," is a historical treasure that may be reached by boat.

6. **Calanques National Park**: The Calanques are a natural treasure with beautiful turquoise seas, limestone cliffs, and good hiking options.

7. **La Corniche**: A lovely coastal route that provides access to various charming beaches as well as stunning views.

8. **Palais Longchamp**: This magnificent structure has a museum as well as a

beautifully designed park that is ideal for a leisurely **stroll.**

9. **Fort St. Jean**: The fort, an ancient military fortification, is now part of MuCEM and offers a blend of history and modern architecture.
10. **Cathédrale de la Major**: A magnificent 19th-century cathedral with beautiful mosaics and breathtaking architecture.
11. **The Old Charity**: This architectural gem, which was once a benevolent almshouse, today houses museums and cultural centres.
12. **Parc Borély**: A picturesque park with botanical gardens, a lake, and a charming château that provides an idyllic getaway from the city.
13. **Stade Vélodrome**: Seeing a football match at this renowned stadium, which is home to Olympique de Marseille, is an amazing experience for sports fans.

14. **Les Terrasses du Port**: A sophisticated shopping and leisure complex ideal for retail therapy while admiring the coastal vistas.
15. **Vallon des Auffes** is a lovely fishing community with colourful boats, charming eateries, and a laid-back ambiance, perfect for a relaxing afternoon.

Discounts And Information On Sightseeing Passes

- **Marseille City Pass**: This pass provides free admission to 22 of the city's most popular attractions, including the Mucem, the Old Port, and Notre-Dame de la Garde. It also comes with unlimited public transportation, a free walking tour, and savings on other activities. The pass is valid for 24 hours, 48 hours, or 72 hours.

- **Marseille Pass**: Like the City Pass, this pass includes a boat ride to the Calanques and a visit to the Château d'If. The pass is only good for two or three days.
- **Marseille Pass Liberté**: The most flexible choice, as it provides you a certain amount of credit to spend on activities and attractions. The credit can be used to visit any of the attractions included in the City Pass or the Marseille Pass, as well as to book tours, buy souvenirs, or eat at restaurants. The pass is good for two, three, or four days.

The cost of sightseeing passes varies according to their validity period and type. Marseille City Passes are available for €25 for 24 hours, €40 for 48 hours, and €55 for 72 hours. Marseille Pass is €45 for two days and €55 for three days.

Marseille Pass Liberté is €35 for two days, €45 for three days, and €55 for four days.

Sailing And Boat Tours In Marseille

Marseille sailing & boat trips provide a variety of options to meet every traveler's preferences. There's something for everyone, whether you're an adrenaline junkie, a relaxed adventurer, or a history buff. Set sail on a classic wooden sailing boat, a sleek modern yacht, or a beautiful catamaran. Local guides will join you, providing depth to your visit by offering fascinating anecdotes about the city's heritage, nautical traditions, and stunning coastal vistas.

Admire the breathtaking panoramas of the Old Port, a lively centre of activity lined with small cafés and old buildings, as you glide through the gentle waves. A magnificent backdrop is provided by the historic Notre-Dame de la

Garde Basilica, which is set on a hill. Another must-see is the gorgeous Calanques National Park, with its rocky limestone cliffs and quiet bays.

If you're lucky, you might see playful dolphins swimming alongside your boat, generating amazing moments and memories. Many trips also include swimming and snorkelling stops, allowing you to cool off and immerse yourself in the Mediterranean's crystal-clear waters.

As the sun begins to set, bask in the warm glow and watch the cityscape turn into a lovely scene. Sip a drink of local wine, eat some typical Marseille food, and soak in the serene atmosphere of the sea.

Sailing and boat trips in Marseille are a must-do if you want to visit this beautiful coastal city and leave with fond recollections of an exciting nautical journey on the Mediterranean waves. Set sail and allow Marseille's maritime enchantment to envelop you!

Beaches And Water Sports In Marseille

The combination of golden dunes, blue waters, and a mild climate makes it a sanctuary for both beachgoers and water sports enthusiasts.

The Plage du Prado, which stretches for several kilometres down the coastline, is one of Marseille's most popular beaches. Because to its excellent sand and shallow waters, it is great for families and people looking for a leisurely dip in the sea. The Plage de la Pointe Rouge, located nearby, has a bustling environment with beach clubs and water sports facilities. Visitors can enjoy activities like kayaking, paddleboarding, and windsurfing while taking advantage of the sea's mild waves.

The Calanques, a series of stunning limestone cliffs and coves, offer a unique coastal experience for those looking for a more isolated vacation. These pristine natural beauties, only accessible by boat or hiking, provide an unsurpassed environment for swimming and snorkelling in crystal-clear waters.

The shoreline of Marseille also draws thrill-seekers looking for adrenaline-pumping water sports. Kitesurfing and jet skiing are popular activities, and a variety of courses and rental shops cater to both novice and experienced riders. The region's strong Mistral wind provides great conditions for kite-based activities, making it a popular destination for adrenaline addicts.

Furthermore, Marseille's diverse marine life makes it an appealing destination for scuba diving. Divers of all skill levels can explore underwater caves, vivid reefs, and sunken ships at a variety of dive sites. The Calanques National Park, which covers both land and marine environments, has some of the most breathtaking dive locations in the region.

Hiking And Treking In Calanques

The Calanques, a series of small and steep-walled inlets, make for an unforgettable trekking experience. The varied pathways appeal to a wide range of fitness levels, from leisurely strolls to strenuous treks, making it accessible to people of all ages and abilities. As you explore this Mediterranean treasure, you'll be rewarded with panoramic views that are nothing short of breathtaking.

The Calanques will captivate you whether you choose the conventional coastal paths that provide glimpses of the dazzling Mediterranean at every turn or the more difficult walks that lead you up to lofty viewing points. With each step, you'll meet a distinct blend of scents from the landscape's pine trees, thyme, and wildflowers.

The marine life in the Calanques' beautiful waters is equally attractive. Many people enjoy snorkelling or diving after a refreshing walk to discover the bright underwater world filled with colourful species and unique marine flora.

Keep an eye out for local wildlife like the majestic Griffon vultures and endangered species that find refuge in this protected region as you walk the rocky trails. Respect for the environment and responsible tourism are critical to sustaining the Calanques' sensitive ecosystem.

To get the most out of your hiking experience, go during the shoulder seasons of spring and autumn, when the weather is nice and the trails are less busy. Following safety guidelines and securing appropriate permissions also assures a smooth and enjoyable journey.

Hiking and trekking in the Calanques National Park is an invigorating experience that links you to nature's raw beauty. So take your rucksack and hiking boots, and go out to discover the riches of this Mediterranean paradise.

Cycling Routes

- **Corniche Kennedy**: The Corniche Kennedy is a popular bicycle path in Marseille. This gorgeous route, which runs along the coast, provides bikers with breathtaking views of the azure Mediterranean waves, craggy cliffs, and attractive beach cottages. The nice sea wind and dynamic environment make it an absolute treat for riders, whether they are looking for a relaxing ride or a demanding workout.
- **Parc Balnéaire du Prado**: The Parc Balnéaire du Prado provides a

well-maintained and safe cycle path for people looking for a family-friendly cycling experience. Its lush flora, sandy beaches, and recreational facilities make it a popular destination for both bikers and non-cyclists. The park's level topography accommodates cyclists of all ages, making it a great location for a peaceful ride with family and friends.

- **Calanques National Park**: Bicyclists looking for adventure will find heaven in the Calanques National Park. This rocky and wild environment, located just outside the city, offers tough courses that reward bikers with breathtaking vistas of limestone cliffs, secret coves, and crystal-clear waters. The park's varied topography allows bikers to explore a variety of pathways, ranging from easy to difficult.

- **Vieux Port to Notre-Dame de la Garde**: The route from Vieux Port to Notre-Dame de la Garde is a must-try for a cultural and historical cycling adventure. This landmark hilltop church provides a breathtaking perspective of Marseille and its surrounds. The ascent may be difficult, but the views and the spectacular design of the basilica make it all worthwhile.
- **Îles du Frioul**: A bicycle excursion to Îles du Frioul will take you on an island-hopping journey. Cyclists may explore these gorgeous islands, famed for their pristine beaches and quiet environment, by taking a ferry from the Vieux Port. The flat and well-marked paths on the islands make for a leisurely ride, and visitors can also sample the local cuisine and take up the Mediterranean atmosphere.

Marseille has an ever-expanding network of bike pathways around the city and its suburbs as riding gains popularity as an eco-friendly and health-conscious means of transportation. Visitors and locals alike may enjoy Marseille's diverse beauty, which ranges from busy metropolitan streets to tranquil coastline settings. So take a bike, put on a helmet, and immerse yourself in the wonderful cycling experience that this enchanting city has to offer.

Itinerary For 3 Days

Day 1:

- **Morning**: Begin your day in Marseille by visiting the magnificent Basilique Notre-Dame de la Garde. This beautiful church, perched on a hilltop, offers panoramic views of the city and the Mediterranean Sea. Take in the gorgeous scenery and see the ornate buildings.

- **Afternoon**: Visit Marseille's famous Vieux-Port (Old Port), the core of the city's nautical legacy. Stroll down the seaside promenade and stop in one of the many charming cafés or restaurants for a fantastic seafood lunch. You can also see the city from the sea by taking a boat excursion.
- **Evening**: Explore Le Panier's cosmopolitan neighbourhood. Explore its narrow alleyways, which are adorned with colourful architecture, fashionable boutiques, and brilliant street art. Visit La Vieille Charité, a former almshouse turned cultural centre and museum.

Day 2:
- **Morning**: Visit the Marseille History Museum, which is located in the Centre Bourse. Learn about the city's history,

including its Greek and Roman origins and evolution over time.

- **Afternoon**: Take in the colourful ambiance of the Cours Julien, which is famed for its artistic and bohemian vibes. Explore art galleries, eccentric stores, and a trendy cafe for a light lunch.
- **Evening**: Pay a visit to the Mucem (Museum of European and Mediterranean Civilizations), an architectural marvel with a view of the sea. Explore the intriguing exhibitions that highlight the Mediterranean region's rich cultural heritage.

Day 3:

- **Morning**: Take a short boat ride to the Château d'If, a historic stronghold on a small island off Marseille's coast. This infamous location served as the inspiration for Alexandre Dumas' novel

"The Count of Monte Cristo." Explore the fortress and take in the views of the sea.

- **Afternoon**: Relax on one of Marseille's magnificent beaches, such as Plage des Catalans or Plage du Prado. Bask in the sun, cool off in the Mediterranean, or try some water sports.
- **Evening**: Finish your three-day trip in Marseille with a stroll down the Corniche Kennedy, a gorgeous beachfront boulevard. As the sun goes down, you'll be treated to spectacular views of the sea and the city skyline.

Itinerary For 7 Days

Day 1: Arrival and orientation in Marseille

Begin your tour by strolling along the famous Vieux Port (Old Port) after arriving and settling into your accommodation. Admire the lovely boats and lively environment while dining at a small café on classic French cuisine. Don't miss out on seeing the magnificent Notre-Dame de la Garde Basilica, which offers breathtaking panoramic views of the city.

Day 2: Visit the Historic Sites of Marseille

Today, embark on a historical tour of Marseille. To learn more about the city's rich cultural legacy, go to the MuCEM (Museum of European and Mediterranean Civilizations). Explore the historic district of Le Panier, which is home to lovely streets, artisan stores, and small cafes, as well as the historical Fort Saint-Jean. Finish your day with a stroll down the Corniche, a lovely beachfront road with breathtaking views of the Mediterranean Sea.

Calanques National Park on Day 3

Spend the day visiting Calanques National Park's natural treasures. Hike or take a boat tour to the Calanques, which have stunning limestone cliffs and turquoise coves ideal for swimming and snorkelling. Don't forget to bring your camera to capture the stunning scenery of this one-of-a-kind coastal location.

Aix-en-Provence on Day 4 Day Out

Travel to Aix-en-Provence, a lovely town known for its art, culture, and vibrant markets. Explore the scenic neighbourhoods, pay a visit to Cours Mirabeau, and learn about the hometown of renowned painter Paul Cézanne. In one of the numerous lovely restaurants, sample the local Provençal food.

Day 5: The Modern Side of Marseille

Visit La Joliette and the Les Docks Village, two sophisticated shopping and leisure districts in Marseille. Visit the Mucem rooftop terrace for beautiful views and a soothing atmosphere. If you enjoy history, you should go to Château d'If, the famed island fortification from Alexandre Dumas' "The Count of Monte Cristo."

Day 6: Cultural Immersion

Spend the day immersed in the cultural environment of Marseille. Admire a variety of artistic masterpieces at the Musée des Beaux-Arts and the Museum of Contemporary Art. Attend a musical or theatrical production at the Opéra de Marseille or one of the city's many theatres.

Day 7: Beaches and Goodbye

Spend the day relaxing on one of Marseille's beautiful beaches, such as Plage des Catalans or Prado Beach. Soak up the sun, swim in the Mediterranean, and enjoy the peace and quiet. In the evening, savour the last moments of your memorable Marseille journey with a farewell meal at a local restaurant.

CHAPTER 6: MARSEILLE SHOPPING

Overview Of The Marseille Shopping Scene

The Old Port (Vieux Port) neighbourhood is one of the highlights of Marseille's shopping experience. Visitors can walk down the quayside and discover a plethora of traditional markets and stalls selling local items, artisanal crafts, and fresh fruit. The fish market is especially enjoyable, providing an insight into the region's maritime past as well as culinary delights.

Rue Paradis is a must-see for anybody interested in luxury shopping. This upmarket strip, lined with high-end boutiques and recognised designer stores, caters to fashion fans looking for the latest trends and exclusive collections. A short distance away, La Canebière Avenue provides a more varied shopping experience with a mix of mainstream and local boutiques.

Marseille is also recognised for its diverse neighbourhoods, each with their own particular commercial character. The city's oldest area, Le Panier, exudes a bohemian vibe, with quirky stores and vintage boutiques selling everything from retro couture to unique gifts. The chic Cours Julien district, on the other hand, is an artistic refuge with numerous cool retailers, art galleries, and concept shops.

Marseille also has several sophisticated shopping centres for customers looking for retail therapy all under one roof. Les Terrasses du Port, with its spectacular waterfront setting, and the Centre Bourse, located in the city's core, both provide a diverse selection of stores, restaurants, and entertainment venues.

Suggestions For Marseille Shopping

- **The Old Port**: Marseille's most popular shopping district, with a wide range of businesses including souvenir shops, clothes stores, and jewellery stores. Prices in this area are normally on the higher side.
- **Canebière**: This is another major shopping street in Marseille, with a mix of high-end and low-cost stores. Prices vary according to the shop.

- **Noailles Market**: This is an excellent location for purchasing fresh produce, spices, and other Mediterranean delicacies. Prices are extremely inexpensive here.
- **Les Accates** is a chic Marseille neighbourhood with a variety of individual boutiques. Prices in this area may be slightly higher than in other sections of the city.
- **La Plaine** is a vibrant Marseille neighbourhood with a variety of cafés, restaurants, and shops. Prices are normally on the low side.

10 Must-Buy Souvenirs

1. **Marseille soap** is a traditional soap prepared from olive oil and herbs. It's a terrific way to bring a little bit of the

South of France home with you. Prices begin about €5.

2. **Navettes**: These are little almond pastries that are a Marseille speciality. They're a tasty and popular souvenir. Prices begin around €1 per navette.

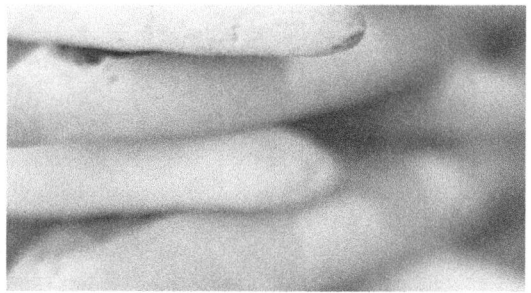

3. **Calissons d'Aix:** These are almond-based sweets from the nearby city of Aix-en-Provence. They're a tasty and popular souvenir. A box of 12 calissons starts at roughly €5.

4. **Herbes de Provence**: This is a herb blend used in Provençal cooking. It's a terrific way to bring the flavours of the South of France home with you. Prices for a small jar start about €5.

5. **Pastis** is a popular anise-flavored liquor from Marseille. It's an excellent gift for folks who appreciate exploring new cocktails. A bottle starts about €10 in price.

6. **Lavender products:** Because lavender is a symbol of Provence, it makes an excellent keepsake. Lavender items come in a variety of shapes and sizes, ranging from soaps and lotions to sachets and potpourri. Prices begin about €5.

7. **books by Marcel Pagnol**: Born in Marseille, this famous French author's writings are a terrific opportunity to discover more about the city and its

culture. Paperbacks start around €10 in price.

8. **Postcards**: Because Marseille is such a lovely city, postcards are an excellent way to remember your visit. Postcards are available at most souvenir shops and are a reasonably priced keepsake. Prices for postcards begin about €0.50.

9. **T-shirts**: Because Marseille has a thriving street art movement, T-shirts

with photos of the city's most famous murals are a popular souvenir. T-shirts are available in most souvenir shops and are a reasonably priced keepsake. T-shirts start around €10 in price.

10. **Keychains**: A terrific way to commemorate your trip to Marseille is with a keychain. Keychains with photos of the city's most prominent landmarks, such as the Old Port and Notre-Dame de la Garde, are available. Prices for keychains start around €2.

Tips For Saving Money And Avoiding Tourist Traps

- **Off-Season Travel**: Visit Marseille during the shoulder seasons (spring and fall), when the weather is still pleasant but lodging and attractions are less expensive than during the busy summer months.
- **Public Transportation**: Take use of Marseille's excellent public transportation system, which includes buses and trams and provides cost-effective alternatives to explore the

city and adjacent attractions. Consider getting a day pass for limitless travel.

- **Instead visiting pricey hotels in the city centre, look for budget-friendly options** such as hostels, guesthouses, or vacation rentals in residential neighbourhoods. You may immerse yourself in the local culture while saving money this way.
- **Avoid touristic meals near key sites** in favour of real local eateries. Marseille is famous for its great street cuisine, such as panisses and socca, which provide a delightful and inexpensive way to quench your appetite.
- **Free and low-cost activities**: Take in the natural beauty and historical monuments of the city without paying a fortune. Stroll around Marseille's historic Vieux Port, visit the landmark Notre-Dame de la Garde for panoramic views, and

discover Le Panier, the city's oldest neighbourhood.

- **Consider obtaining a Marseille City Pass**, which provides free or discounted entry to different sites, public transport, and guided tours.
- **Picnics and Markets**: Get a taste of the local way of life by shopping for fresh vegetables and regional delicacies at Marseille's markets. For a low-cost and pleasurable supper, take a picnic to one of the parks or by the water.
- **Keep an Eye Out for Scams**: As with any tourist location, keep an eye out for scams or pickpocketing in crowded areas. Keep your valuables safe and avoid street vendors who sell costly items.

CHAPTER 7: MARSEILLE'S NIGHTLIFE IS EXCITING

Marseille's nightlife is concentrated in its many neighbourhoods, each with its own distinct and vibrant vibe. With its lively taverns and waterfront clubs, the Vieux Port is a popular starting place for revellers. The Cours Julien sector comes alive with creative flair as the night develops, attracting a younger clientele to its fashionable taverns and live music establishments.

Marseille's nightlife cannot be discussed without discussing the city's passion of music and dance. The city's live music culture is growing, with performances ranging from jazz to electronic beats. Live concerts and DJ sets can be enjoyed in private settings as well as larger clubs that cater to all tastes.

Marseille's nightlife is highlighted by its abundance of rooftop pubs and terraces, which provide not only tasty cocktails but also stunning views of the city and the Mediterranean Sea. It's an unforgettable experience to sip a beverage while watching the city lights dazzle below.

The French tradition of late-night dining adds to the attractiveness of Marseille's nightlife. Following a night of partying, locals and visitors alike go to the city's many late-night eateries to savour delectable delicacies, ensuring that the night's excitement continues into the early hours.

Live Music Venues

- **Le Moulin**, a historic theatre that has hosted performances since the 1950s, is one of the city's most prominent live music venues. It has become a favourite venue for both local and international artists due to its small environment and great acoustics. The eclectic programme at the venue includes everything from rock and jazz to electronic and hip-hop, guaranteeing that there is something for everyone.
- **L'Embobineuse** is a must-see for those looking for a more alternative and underground experience. This out-of-the-ordinary venue in the bohemian Cours Julien neighbourhood hosts experimental music, indie bands, and avant-garde performances. Its grungy charm and commitment to

promoting upcoming performers have earned it a distinct place in Marseille's music community.

- **Espace Julien**, on the other hand, is a multi-functional space that accommodates concerts, club nights, and cultural events. Because of its vast capacity, it can host larger performances, attracting major acts from France and beyond. Music fans flock here to see remarkable performances in a dynamic setting.

- **L'Affranchi** is a popular pick for enthusiasts of world music. This venue promotes global musical influences and develops a welcoming community feel with its diverse programme of reggae, world fusion, and traditional sounds.

Nightclubs and Dance Spots

- **The Old Port region** in the city's heart comes alive after dark, with a diverse mix of nightclubs bordering the riverfront. Everything from upmarket lounges to underground techno havens may be found here. Le Moulin, a historic venue, organises a variety of concerts and DJ performances, attracting both residents and tourists.

- **For a more intimate experience, visit the Cours Julien neighbourhood.** This trendy and artsy neighbourhood is home to tiny dance clubs where you can groove to alternative beats and discover new artists. The environment is bright and relaxed, making it a perfect place to socialise and meet new people.

- **Electronic music fans** will be thrilled to learn that the city is home to several renowned techno clubs. These venues, ranging from the iconic Cabaret Aléatoire to the industrial-themed Dock des Suds, often feature internationally acclaimed DJs, establishing Marseille as a prominent destination on the electronic music circuit.

- **La Friche la Belle de Mai** is a must-see for a sample of the city's unique culture. This cultural complex holds a variety of events, such as dance parties and festivals, that highlight Marseille's artistic character and multifaceted identity.

Marseille's nightlife is not limited to classic nightclubs. Rooftop bars with panoramic views of the metropolitan skyline are becoming increasingly popular. These hip hangouts offer a refined setting for enjoying cocktails under the starry Mediterranean sky.

Theater and Performing Art

The city's theatre culture provides a varied choice of performances that appeal to both locals and visitors. The magnificent Marseille Opera House, built in the 18th century, is a tribute to the city's dedication to the arts. The opera house, known for its beautiful architecture and world-class productions, continues to stage operas, ballets, and classical concerts, enthralling audiences with its majesty and artistic prowess.

Aside from the opera, Marseille has a plethora of theatres and performing arts facilities to suit a wide range of tastes. The city gives a forum for artists to explore and express their talents, from traditional French plays to experimental and avant-garde acts. The lively theatre sector, particularly in the Vieux-Port region, pulsates with the energy of actors, musicians, and dancers, providing an invigorating atmosphere for art lovers.

Furthermore, the city takes pride in conserving Provençal culture through folkloric performances and regional plays that connect modern audiences with their cultural legacy. Local festivals and events, such as the Festival de Marseille, boost the city's cultural standing by showcasing varied international artists and encouraging cultural interchange.

Marseille has a robust street performing culture in addition to theatre shows. The city's broad spaces and vibrant streets frequently serve as impromptu platforms for skilled street performers, enriching the everyday lives of both inhabitants and visitors.

In Marseille, theatre and performing arts are used not just for entertainment but also for cultural expression, communication, and social reflection. The city's unwavering dedication to artistic endeavours has cemented its image as a dynamic and culturally rich destination for theatregoers and artists alike.

Bars And Pubs

The characteristic Provencal charm of Marseille's taverns and pubs is one of its most enticing features. Many of these places exhibit a laid-back Mediterranean attitude and welcome guests with friendly friendliness. Traditional pubs, sophisticated lounges, and modern rooftop bars dot the city, offering a diverse selection of locations in which to have a drink or two.

Pastis, an anise-flavored liqueur that symbolises the region's cultural past, is the local beverage of choice in Marseille. The clinking of glasses filled with this popular aperitif reverberates throughout the city as the sun sets over the ancient harbour, producing a time-honored rite enjoyed by locals.

Wandering through Marseille's old streets reveals a plethora of hidden jewels - cosy, family-run eateries that have been serving consumers for decades. These intimate settings provide an authentic experience, allowing guests to immerse themselves in the city's customs and connect with its welcoming citizens.

For those looking for a more modern environment, the city's modern bars and pubs cater to a wide range of tastes. Live music venues showcase great local artists, adding to the lively atmosphere. Beer fans can also enjoy the city's growing number of craft brewers, which showcase the city's expanding culinary prowess.

Marseille's bars and pubs are more than just places to drink; they also serve as vital social hubs, promoting connections between people from all walks of life. Conversations flow freely, laughter rings forth, and friendships emerge naturally. Strangers often become friends by the end of the night, connected by their shared experience of Marseille's enthralling nightlife.

CHAPTER 8: RECOGNIZING FOREIGN TRANSACTION FEES

- **Consider Your Bank's Policies**: Before departing, call your bank or credit card issuer to learn about their overseas transaction fees. Some financial institutions offer cards tailored exclusively for international travel, with cheaper or waived foreign transaction costs.
- **Choose Local Currency**: When making a transaction with your credit card, always choose to be charged in the local currency (Euros in France) rather than your home currency. This can assist you in avoiding dynamic currency conversion

fees, which are frequently associated with unfavourable exchange rates.

- **ATM Withdrawals**: If you want to withdraw cash from an ATM, be aware that both your bank and the local ATM operator may charge foreign transaction fees. To reduce these fees, consider making fewer, larger withdrawals.
- **Use Fee-Free Cards**: Some credit card firms provide no-fee overseas transaction solutions. Consider getting one of these cards before your trip to Marseille to avoid paying extra fees.
- **Examine Receipts and Statements**: Examine your receipts after each transaction and your card statements on a regular basis for any unexpected fees or anomalies.

Avoid Paying Cell Phone Roaming Fees.

- **Purchase a Local SIM Card**: When arriving in Marseille, consider purchasing a local SIM card. Many mobile providers provide low-cost prepaid SIM cards with data, text, and phone call bundles. This option allows you to use a local phone and data plan rather than roaming.
- **Check with Your Carrier:** Before leaving, contact your home carrier to inquire about foreign plans or temporary roaming packages. Some providers have special offerings that can help you save money on roaming fees while travelling abroad.
- **Connect to Wi-Fi**: There are numerous cafes, restaurants, hotels, and public locations in Marseille that offer free

Wi-Fi. Connect your phone to Wi-Fi networks whenever feasible to prevent using mobile data.

- **Instead of sending ordinary text messages or making international calls, use messaging apps** such as WhatsApp, Viber, or Telegram. These apps use internet data, which is not subject to roaming fees.
- **Offline Maps and Apps**: Before leaving your hotel or any other Wi-Fi-enabled location, download offline maps and critical travel apps that do not require constant internet connectivity. This allows you to navigate without consuming costly data.
- **Enable Aeroplane Mode**: When you're not actively using your phone, put it in aeroplane mode to avoid accidental data consumption or incoming calls that could result in roaming fees.

- **If obtaining a local SIM card is not an option, check with your home carrier for roaming passes** or trip packages designed to lower roaming expenses in certain countries, such as France.

Map Download For Offline Use

To make the most of your vacation, having a downloadable map on your device for offline usage is an excellent tool that will assist you in confidently navigating the city.

Step 1: Select a Reliable Map App

Begin by selecting a reliable map application with offline mapping capability. Google Maps, Maps.me, and CityMaps2Go are all popular options. You can use these apps to download maps for a specific location and access them without an internet connection.

Step 2: Get the Marseille Map.

Before you go, open your preferred map application and search for "Marseille." When the city appears on the screen, check for a link to download the map for offline usage. You may be able to download the full city or particular parts within it, depending on the programme.

Step 3: Check the Completeness of the Map

When the download is finished, double-check that the map contains all of the areas in Marseille that you wish to visit. Check that significant sites, attractions, streets, and public transport routes can be seen on the offline map.

Step 4: Become acquainted with the app's features.

Take some time to investigate the map application's features. Experiment with zooming in and out, putting pins to highlight specific locations, and getting more information about points of interest. Familiarising yourself with these elements will make offline exploration of Marseille easier.

Step 5: Experiment with the Offline Mode

Turn off your mobile data and Wi-Fi before embarking on your excursion to ensure that the offline mode functions properly. Even without an internet connection, the map should still function properly, delivering precise directions.

Learn The Fundamentals Of The Language.

While French is the official language of Marseille and is widely spoken throughout the city, the people have a distinct accent and a distinct collection of idioms that distinguish their speech. It's known as "Marseillais," and it reflects the city's rich cosmopolitan background, which is inspired by its Mediterranean setting and historical connections.

You may notice some unusual words and phrases at first, but don't worry; embracing this local dialect will lead to more honest encounters and a deeper understanding of Marseille's character. Engaging with locals with simple greetings such as "Bonjour" (Hello) or "Merci" (Thank you) is always appreciated, but adding a bit of local flavour will certainly win you some smiles.

Begin by becoming acquainted with common Marseillais terms such as "Fada" (crazy, fun person) and "Boumba" (small child). Don't be afraid to ask locals about definitions and pronunciation; they'll be delighted to share their language and culture with you.

Marseille's cuisine is as well-known as its language, so before eating at a local restaurant, learn the names of some traditional dishes. "Bouillabaisse," a delectable fish stew, and "Panisse," a chickpea flour delicacy, are just two of the menu's must-order items.

The Cost Of Cash At The Airport Is High.

When travelling for business or pleasure, having access to cash is essential for a variety of expenses such as transportation, food, and unexpected emergencies. However, using cash at the airport might be a costly and cumbersome option.

For starters, airport currency exchange facilities frequently demand exorbitant fees and provide unfavourable conversion rates, resulting in huge losses for travellers. These extra fees can quickly build up and have a substantial influence on one's travel budget. Furthermore, the lack of local banks or ATMs within the airport boundaries makes it difficult to find a better alternative for currency conversion.

Second, there are security issues involved with carrying significant sums of cash. Airports are busy hubs with a steady stream of travellers from all walks of life, making them prime targets for pickpockets and larceny. Carrying large sums of money might make travellers feel unsafe and uncomfortable throughout their journey.

Furthermore, the time spent waiting in large lines at currency exchange counters or looking for an ATM can cause extra delays, especially for individuals on a tight schedule or with connecting flights. This delay can be especially aggravating when time is of the importance and every second counts.

Travellers to Marseille are advised to plan ahead and seek other payment methods to reduce the expense of cash at the airport. Using credit or debit cards with low foreign transaction fees can help you save money on currency conversion and give a more secure way to manage your expenses. Furthermore, informing the bank about the journey destination ahead of time will help to avoid any potential problems with card usage abroad.

CONCLUSION

Tips For A Memorable Trip

- **Embrace the Old Port**: Marseille's ancient harbour, the Vieux Port, is the heart of the city and a great place to start your tour. Stroll around the waterfront, eat delicious seafood at the restaurants, and soak up the bustling environment. For a genuinely authentic experience, visit the fish market in the early morning.

- **Explore the Calanques**: The Calanques National Park, located just outside the city, is a must-see for nature lovers. These breathtaking limestone cliffs and crystal-clear bays provide excellent hiking trails as well as possibilities for swimming and sunbathing.

- **Admire Notre-Dame de la Garde:** This landmark basilica on a hill offers a breathtaking panoramic view of Marseille. Visit this sacred site and learn about its history while admiring the breathtaking views.

- **Enjoy the Local Cuisine**: Marseille is well-known for its exquisite cuisine, which is largely inspired by Mediterranean flavours. Try the famous fish stew bouillabaisse, as well as other local delights like pastis, panisse, and socca. Because of the city's diverse population, you may also enjoy superb North African and Middle Eastern cuisine.

- **Engage the Locals**: The people of Marseille are kind, friendly, and proud of their city's history. Engage in talks with the locals, learn a few simple French phrases, and you'll discover that people are eager to assist and share their advice.

- **Visit the MuCEM and Other Museums**: Marseille is home to a number of intriguing museums. The Museum of European and Mediterranean Civilizations (MuCEM) stands out for its presentation of the region's cultural heritage. Other highlights are the Marseille History Museum and the Fine Arts Museum.
- **Walking** around Marseille's main sites is fun, taking advantage of the city's public transport system can save you time and energy. The metro, buses, and trams are all well-connected and efficient, allowing you to easily travel further afield.
- **Respect Local Customs**: As with any destination, it is critical to be aware of local customs and traditions. When visiting holy sites, dress modestly and avoid loud or disruptive behaviour, especially in residential areas.

Travel Advice And Aditional Resourses

Finally, when it comes to travel advice, it is critical to consider the unique requirements and situations of various sorts of travelers, such as lone travelers, families, and LGBTQ people. While traveling to new places, each group may have different needs and confront different obstacles.

Prioritizing personal safety is critical for lone travelers. Researching the place ahead of time, exchanging travel plans with trusted individuals, and remaining cautious are all key measures. Taking advantage of local resources, such as tourist information centers or hotel concierge services, can provide essential direction and assistance throughout the voyage.

Families should prioritize preparing activities for all members and creating a child-friendly environment. It is critical to determine whether the destination has family-friendly accommodations, attractions, and services. Furthermore, keeping important documents, such as passports and medical information, immediately accessible is critical in case of an emergency.

It is critical for LGBTQ visitors to research the destination's cultural and legal context in terms of LGBTQ rights. Familiarizing oneself with local norms and legislation can assist in navigating potential obstacles. Connecting with LGBTQ travel communities, both online and in person, can provide useful information, recommendations, and support.

For all types of travelers, contact information and other tools are vital. Compiling a list of emergency contacts, including local authorities, embassies or consulates, and travel insurance providers, is vital prior to the journey. Additionally, using travel apps, online forums, and destination-specific guidebooks can provide useful information and recommendations.

Travelers can improve their safety, enjoyment, and overall experience by adapting travel guidance to the needs of lone travelers, families, and LGBTQ individuals. Adapting to the specific needs of each group promotes a more inclusive and fulfilling travel experience for all.

Appendix

Maps of Marseille

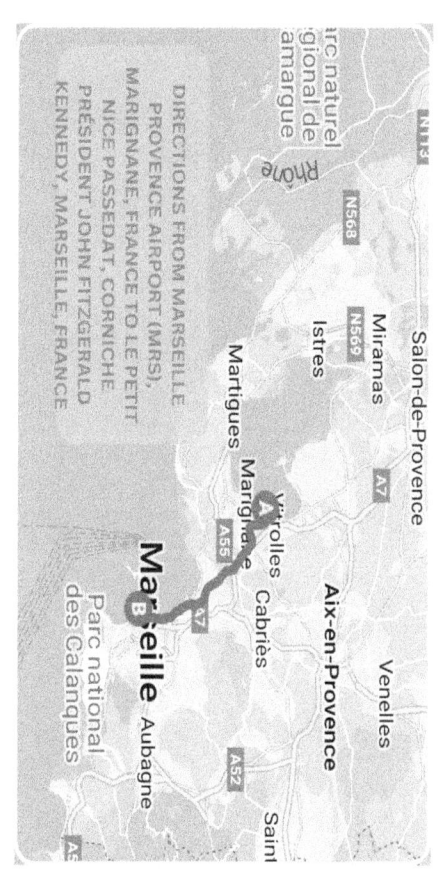

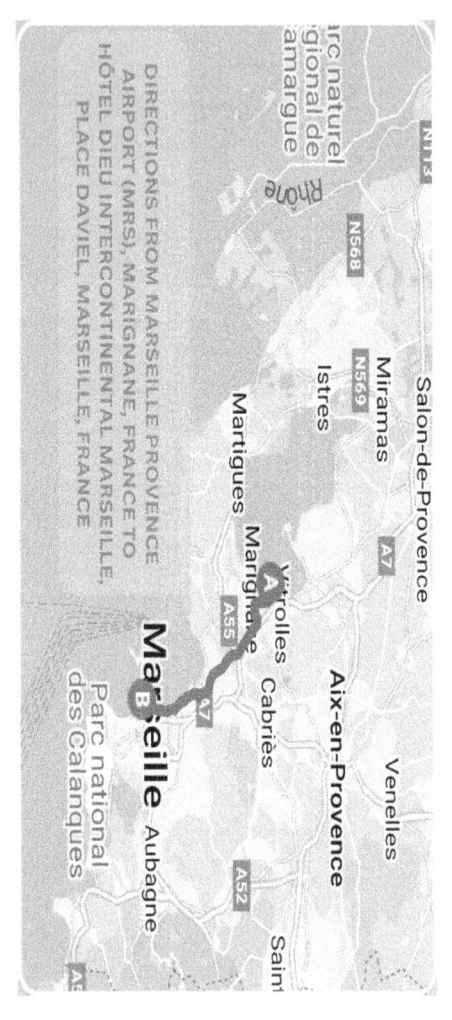

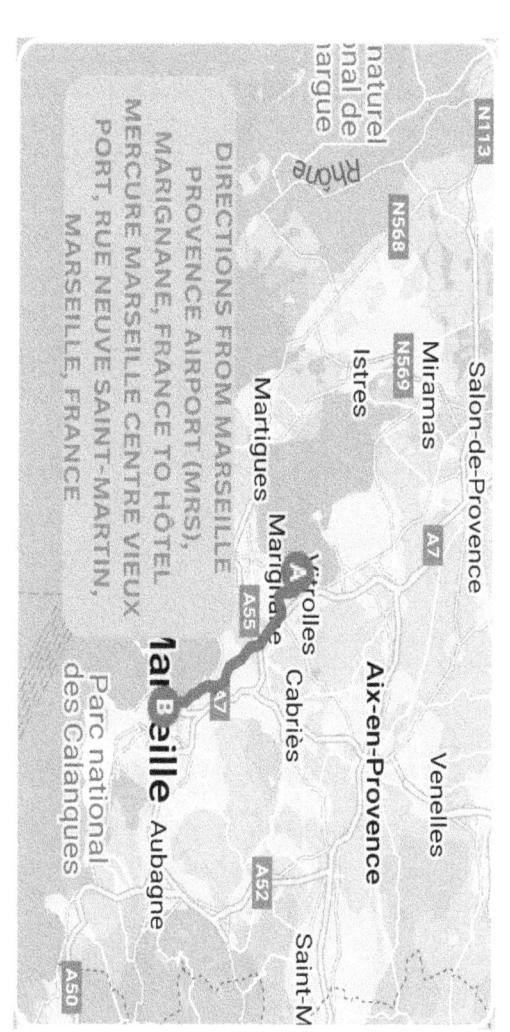

DIRECTIONS FROM MARSEILLE PROVENCE AIRPORT (MRS), MARIGNANE, FRANCE TO HÔTEL MERCURE MARSEILLE CENTRE VIEUX PORT, RUE NEUVE SAINT-MARTIN, MARSEILLE, FRANCE

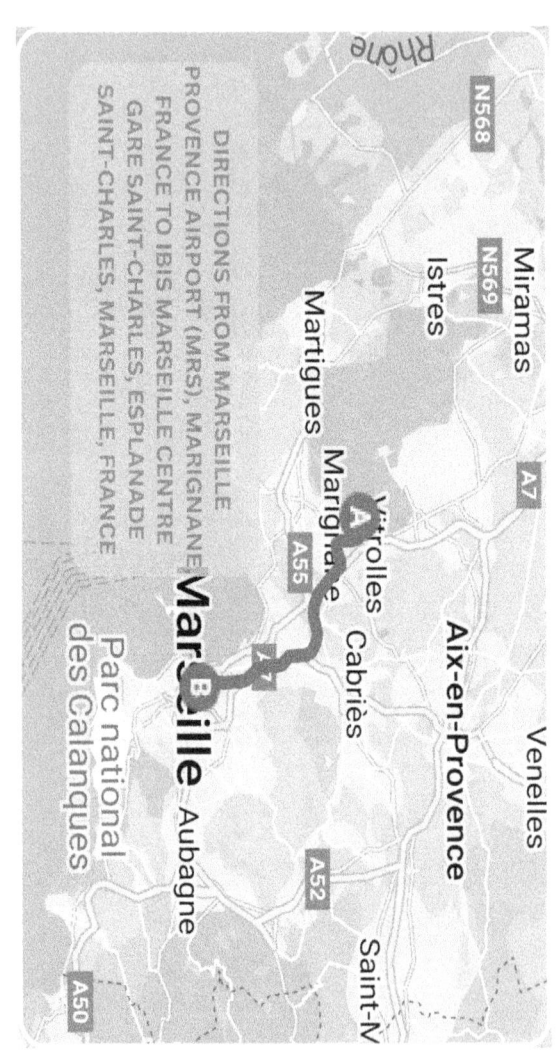

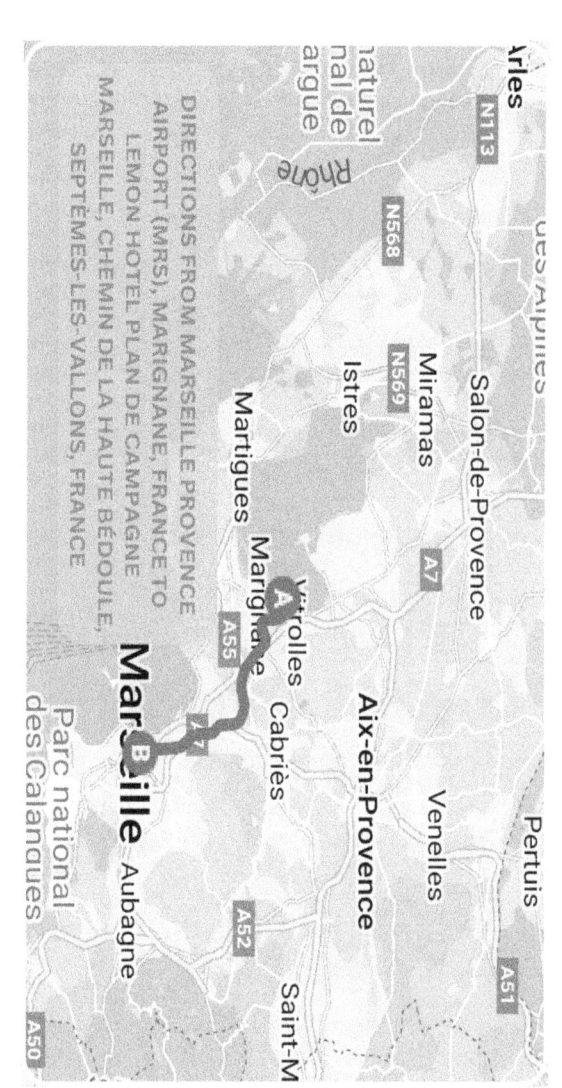

DIRECTIONS FROM MARSEILLE PROVENCE AIRPORT (MRS), MARIGNANE, FRANCE TO LEMON HOTEL PLAN DE CAMPAGNE MARSEILLE, CHEMIN DE LA HAUTE BÉDOULE, SEPTÈMES-LES-VALLONS, FRANCE

DIRECTIONS FROM MARSEILLE PROVENCE AIRPORT (MRS), MARIGNANE, FRANCE TO HÔTEL DES MOULINS, TRAVERSE DES CHARMETTES, ALLAUCH, FRANCE